"Amy Wise's book of quotes will take you on a journey to your best self, enabling you to change your heart and the hearts of those around you. Timely, thought-provoking, and reflective... this is the way to begin your day."

~Elizabeth Geitz, author of *I Am That Child*

"Reading this book is like getting the perfect pep talk from your most trusted friend. These beautiful words will inspire, encourage and empower you, and will give you the confidence to make all your dreams come true. Amy's last name is 'Wise' for a reason!"

~Lois Alter Mark, co-founder of *StyleSubstanceSoul.com*

"Amy Wise lifts us up by reminding us that we are all—each one of us—part of a universal gathering of the heart. Through her carefully chosen words, she sprinkles hope on every page, acknowledging us as brothers and sisters. Is it any wonder that we want more of Wise's inspiration? Giving thanks is the least we can do."

~Julie Maloney, director of *WomenReadingAloud.org*

"Tender and heartfelt. A butterfly of a book."

~Ilie Ruby, author of *The Salt God's Daughter*

"Amy Wise has experienced more than her share of adversity and injustice, yet through it all she has remained positive, choosing happiness rather than bitterness. She always has a positive, encouraging word for everyone - including me."

~Hollye Dexter, co-editor of *Dancing at the Shame Prom*

"Amy's book puts you in a positive frame of mind and makes it difficult for you not to do so."

~Zetta Brown, author of *Messalina: Devourer of Men*

"Amy Wise makes it easy for us to start our day with words of wisdom. A great gift from her heart and soul, to all."

~Madge Woods, writer & marketing director, *TheNextFamily.com*

"Amy's book is full of words to encourage you, inspire you, and brighten your day. These are wise words, by a Wise woman. This is a book you will treasure and want to share with everyone you care about!"

~Kim LePiane, spiritual healer

Believe in Yourself
Inspire Others
Spread Joy!

Start your day on a
positive note...

with quotes from
my heart to yours.

Amy Wise

Believe in Yourself
Inspire Others
Spread *Joy*!

This book is dedicated to ~

My husband Jamie and
my daughter Tatiana.
They are my heart
and my inspiration.

# Gratitude

As with all of us, there are so many people in our lives that shape us, help us, teach us, hold us, listen to us and love us. I'm not sure there is enough room in this book to thank everyone, but I'm going to try...

This book and these words would not have been possible without the love and support of my husband Jamie. He is my rock and my soul-mate. To our daughter Tatiana, you inspire me every single day as I watch you make your own dreams come true. Jamie and Tatiana, you two are literally my heart!

To my parents who *chose* me, raised me and saw me through it all...there are not enough thank yous in the world. I love you!

Lori, you listened and loved during everything. I am so blessed that you are not only my sister, but my dear friend.

Miss Corinne, my *Cali mom*...what would life be like without you next door? You are a treasure.

To Dani, my beautiful niece, who always gives her heart and that little something extra special, just because. You are an angel.

*College Kim*...my friend, my spiritual shoulder, my confidant. From college, to Paris, to marriage, to kids, through the ups and the downs...thank you for always being there!

Angela, my old business partner and forever friend...even though we went down different paths, we made it through and came out even stronger.

*Agent Kim*, you believed in my book and you helped me bring it to life with your amazing team and dedication.

To my author, writer and creative friends; Amy Ferris, Richard Jacoby, Kim LePiane, Madge Woods, Hollye Dexter, Kristine Van Raden, Elynne Chaplik-Aleskow, Melanie Eversley, Elizabeth Geitz, Zetta Brown, Lois Alter Mark, Ilie Ruby, and Julie Maloney...you all shared your beautiful feelings about my book. Thank you for kindness, generosity, time, friendship and love.

To everyone who told me they use my quotes to help them get through difficult days...thank you for the inspiration. You touch me to my soul.

Last but not least; to all my other family members, Jamie's family, and my friends that are too many to mention...thank you for enriching my life. I love you all!

**FOREVER GRATEFUL!**

# Introduction

"One of the reasons I married you is because you are one of the strongest women I know. Why are you letting these people destroy you? I want my wife back." Those words were spoken to me by my husband during the darkest time of my life. That moment, and his words, were as some would say, my *aha* moment. From that conversation, came what would end up being this book. My quotes began as a cathartic way for me to deal with a very difficult and unheard of situation.

In 2007 everything I knew came crashing down around me. It was discovered that the water we had been using in our candy/gift store was not drinking water but reclaimed sewer water. Yes, I know, horrible. From illness, to the destruction and closure of our business and dream, to the 5 year fight of our lives against the water department, city, developer and contractor, who all refused to do the right thing, I didn't know how to deal with it all.

After *the moment* with my husband, I began to rethink everything. It was time to get my happy back! Words brought light back into my life. I started writing and haven't stopped since. It's proof that dreams do come true...again! I began to wake up every morning and come up with a quote about what I was feeling in that moment. Eventually I started sharing my personal quotes on the internet and realized I was not only helping myself, but others as well. I started receiving responses from people that said...

"How did you know exactly what I needed to hear today?"

"Your words got me through the day, thank you."

"Your quotes always help me on my bad days."

"I look forward to seeing what your next quote is going to be."

The comments touched me deeply because every word I was coming up with and sharing came from my own personal experiences. I appreciated every response about my quotes, but none as much as those that came from my teenage daughter's friends...

"Whenever I'm having a hard time I read your quotes to help me get through."

"Your quotes help me so much, thank you Mama Wise."

"Your quotes are how I start my day."

"You don't understand how much your quotes help me. Thank you."

"I love your quotes Mama Wise. I read them every day."

I literally cried when I began receiving messages from teens. To be able to make an impact on a young person who is having moments of struggle, well, that is what it is all about. I'm so grateful.

My quotes come from love, friendship, faith, strength, resiliency and determination to get through the difficult times and come out even stronger on the other end. So whether you read this entire book in one sitting or pick it up when you need a lift or positive reminder…just know that every word comes from my heart and each quote is a piece of my soul that I'm now sharing with you.

My hope is that you use this book to help you find your joy, live your dreams and follow your heart!

*Let go of the past.*
*Release the pain.*
*Grab on to now.*
*Live for today!*

~Amy Wise

*Dreams*
become
*reality*
when we
*open our eyes*
and take the
*steps*
to get there.

– Amy Wise

③

Follow
your
heart.
Fill your
life.

—Amy Wise

There's enough room in the garden
   for all of the flowers to bloom.
There's enough room in the sky
   for all of the stars to shine.
There's enough room in the world
   for all of us to grow....TOGETHER!

                 - Amy Wise

*If you don't step into the unknown, how will you ever know?*

– Amy Wise

Diversity is God's artwork.

– Amy Wise

Stuck? Take one step.
Lost? Find a new way.
Broken? Pick up the pieces.
Dreaming?
Make it come true. It is possible.
It all starts with YOU!

– Amy Wise

Obstacles are
mOvable so
NEVER, EVER
let them get in
yOur way!

-Amy Wise

Let go
of fear
and embrace
FIERCE!

- Amy Wise

If you need *help* ask for it, if you don't, *help* someone else.

Give your *heart* to the *world* and make it a *better place.*

—Amy Wise

*Marriage*
isn't about *fantasy*
and *fireworks...*
it's about *friendship*
and *faithfulness.*

— Amy Wise

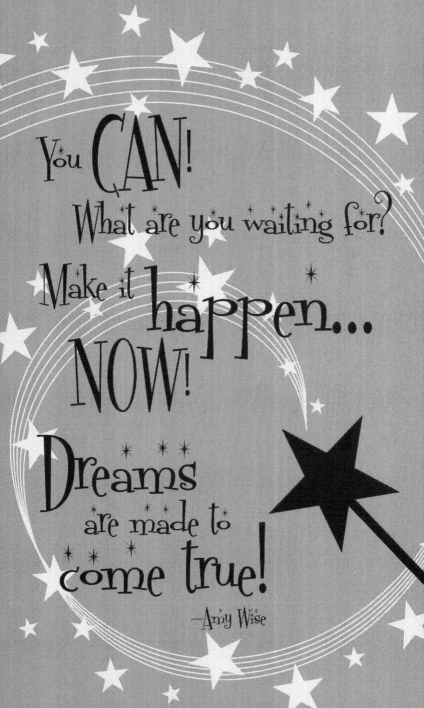

You CAN!
What are you waiting for?
Make it happen...
NOW!
Dreams
are made to
come true!
—Amy Wise

Never underestimate the *power* of *prayer.*
—Amy Wise

Use your **mistakes**
as **lessons learned**
and **experiences** to be
**shared,**

**THEN** you will have
the **wisdom** to **GROW!**

— Amy Wise

Let go
of what you think
"should be"
and allow what "can be"
to change your life.

—Amy Wise

Pay it forward
*every*
single day!

-Amy Wise

When life gets **challenging**,
don't lose **hope**,
take a **deep breath**,
**look** life in the **eye**
and **challenge** it
**right back!**
You're **stronger**
than you know.
**Know that!**

-Amy Wise

*Love* = kindness, respect, communication, partnership, compromise, passion and laughter.

Never settle for less.

If there is less, don't give up, don't walk away...

work on making more...

*together!*

-Amy Wise

Makin' dreams happen.... one day at a time.

—Amy Wise

# Claim amazing!

-Amy Wise

If we hold each other up,
   help each other out
and support each other
   through it all...
then everyone's
   dreams come true.
      -Amy Wise

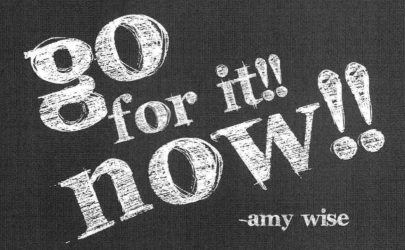

go for it!! now!!
–amy wise

☑ NOW
☐ LATER

Stop –
Close your eyes –
Say a prayer –
Make a wish –

Open your eyes –

Now go –

Start today –
Little by little –
Make your wish
come true.

–Amy Wise

24

What was... *done*.

What is... *precious*.

What will be... *amazing!*

-Amy Wise

It's never too late to
**DREAM.**
It's never too late to
**START OVER.**
It's never too late to
**GO FOR IT...**
**again!**
—Amy Wise

# Aim
## for nothing
## less than
# extraordinary!

*—Amy Wise*

Step out
of your
comfort zone
and make a new zone
comfortable.
—Amy Wise

# soar!

-Amy Wise

If there's a
mountain
in front of you,
climb it!
You'll be
amazed
at what's on the
other
side.
—Amy Wise

Create the
"music"
of your life
by doing
what makes
your heart sing.

–Amy Wise

# Faith
# + Family
# + Friends =

*Fabulousness!*

-Amy Wise

Picture *your* wildest dreams coming true.

Work *patiently toward them.*
*Suddenly, one day,*
*you'll wake up and find*
they aren't dreams
anymore....
they've come true!

–Amy Wise

When you are
*up,*
be the lift for
those around you
that may be
*down.*

—Amy Wise

No more *why...*
only *why not!*

— Amy Wise

Think with your *head.* Follow your *heart.* Fill your *soul.* -Amy Wise

*Friends*
*are like* gold...
*years and years can go by*
*and they become even more of a*
*treasure.*

—*Amy Wise*

Be a
dream
catcher!

-Amy Wise

When things
are bright....
be someone else's light.

- Amy Wise

Don't just step out
of the box....
jUMp & Run!
Then do what fits YOU,
not what fits in
the box!
-Amy Wise

Take a moment
and think of something
in your life that makes you **smile**.
Then take a minute and truly
**appreciate** it.
Pause, rewind, repeat.
Now you're smiling and appreciating over
and over again…it just never ends!

–Amy Wise

If we all
take small steps
to pay it forward,
then nobody has to take
big steps backward.

– Amy Wise

Concentrating on
the positive
lets you soar,

while dwelling on the
negative keeps you
down

you choose...
are you going to
fly or fall?

-Amy Wise

43

Live through **your heart,**
go with **your "gut"**

and decisions
will be **just right**
for **you!**

- Amy Wise

Take a *different* route,
you might just find miracles
around the corner.

– Amy Wise

Work
methodically
toward your
*dream*
and one day
you'll look
around and
realize you're
*living it.*
—Amy Wise

Circumstances
might take you
down but they
can NEVER
prevent you
from getting
back up!

– Amy Wise

If for
no reason at all,
a giant smile comes
across your face and
tears of joy
and gratitude fill
your eyes, you know you're on
the right path.

If for no reason at all, you have
a frown and tears of sadness,
then whatever you do, make sure
you change paths!

It's all up to you!

Go, find what
makes you smile!

—Amy Wise

Never limit yourself, because the possibilities truly are endless.

—Amy Wise

Paths are meant to be **walked**,
  mountains are meant to be **climbed**,
waves are meant to be **surfed**
  and life is meant to be **LIVED!**

Through it all we **become** who we are and
  what we were **meant to be.**

-Amy Wise

There's nothing better
than doing what you love.

Passion is priceless!

-Amy Wise

If you fall,
don't try and get up
by yourself....

reach for
someone's hand.
Then do the same
for someone else
when you're
standing tall.
— Amy Wise

Just when you
think
you can't take
another step,
that's when it's
time to fly!

-Amy Wise

Lead by example.
Live your best life.
Love your spouse.
Hug your child.
Help your neighbor.
Write your truth.
Inspire the next generation.

-Amy Wise

*Wonder, then believe.*

—Amy Wise

Dream BEYOND big!

★Amy Wise

56

*Each of us has the ability to be incredible in all that we do... so go... shine brighter than bright!*

—Amy Wise

When *opportunity*
knocks,
*listen* to your heart,
then do lots of
*research*.

-Amy Wise

see that hurdle
in front of you....
ready,
set,
JUMP!
see that hurdle
in back of you....
it's exactly
where it
should be.

– Amy wise

Words can wound or words can do wonders... speak from your heart.

- Amy Wise

Your dream is just that.... **yours.**
So step out of the box,
   crush it,
      recycle it,
         and go make
**YOUR** dream come true!
- Amy Wise

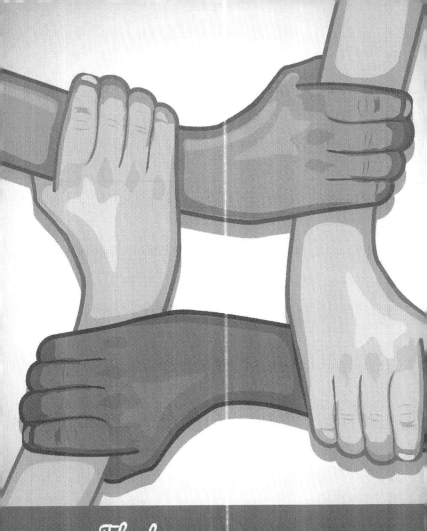

The best way to say,
"Thank you for the help,"
is to pay it forward
any way you can.

- Amy Wise

**Love** begins with you...
love yourself,
**be true** to yourself,
and **love** what you do.
Don't ever forget
there's only
one **YOU!**

— Amy Wise

believe
you can
and you will.

— Amy Wise

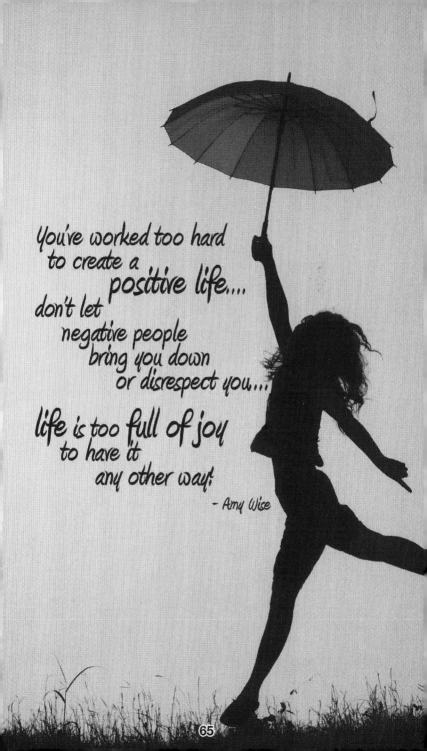

You've worked too hard
  to create a
         positive life...
don't let
     negative people
          bring you down
             or disrespect you...

life is too full of joy
   to have it
        any other way!

— Amy Wise

65

Get up,
get out,
go for it!
-Amy Wise

My dream isn't your dream,
and your dream isn't my dream,
but that doesn't mean
we can't **reach** for
our dreams **together.**

– Amy Wise

start fresh
this very minute,

dream big
this very second,

create
your future
NOW!

-Amy Wise

Choose your path
because it's the road YOU
want to travel.
Follow the direction
that feeds YOUR soul.

-Amy Wise

No regrets... only lessons *learned.*
No shame... only **truths told.**
No hate... only *love.*
No fear... only **excitement.**
No sadness... only **joy.**
No anger... only **kindness.**
Not tomorrow... **TODAY!** —Amy Wise

# Stars
### are in the sky, not on TV.

We all have the ability to shine one way or another.

Where does your light come from?

— Amy Wise

If we all
**open the door**
for someone else,
the whole **world opens**
up to **everyone!**

– Amy Wise

there are a lot of other zones that can make you **comfortable**. go ahead, step out, try another one on for size.... it might just be a **PeRFect Fit**.

-amy wise

73

Praying
+ thanking
+ asking
+ believing
+ working
+ giving
+ loving
_____
= amazing!

-Amy Wise

Yesterday's *choices* are Today's *lessons* and tomorrow's *growth.*

—Amy Wise

*Success* isn't about big bank accounts, titles, fame, climbing ladders, or initials after last names.

*Success* is about *happiness* and *generosity*.

*The rest is just icing on your cake.*

*- Amy Wise*

You decide. You choose.
You create. You define.
YOUR life!

- Cory Wise

77

The path without footprints
might be scary at first,
but the **adventure**
into the **unknown**
is a walk
**worth taking.**

- Amy Wise

Don't dread what you do.
Dream what you want.
Then make it come true!

— Amy Wise

If there's something standing
in the way of your happiness...
pick it up, move it,
walk around it or
jump over it...
it's time to get your
happy back!
– Amy Wise

Don't sit idly by
when instead you
can **Choose**
to **Fly!**

- Amy Wise

Wealth
without giving
is like life
without loving.

- Amy Wise

Are you living your passion
or feeling imprisoned?

Break free and take
the steps to
follow your dream!

— Amy Wise

After you ask,
believe and receive...
make sure to put
it to good use.

-Amy Wise

When you realize
the possibilities
are endless.....
they ARE!

— Amy Wise

Even if life makes you take a step backward...never, ever stop paying it forward.

Rewards of the heart... *priceless.*

- Amy Wise

# YOU ROCK!

Don't ever forget that!

- Amy Wise

*Closed mind* =
*ignorance, fear, judgment & impossibilities.*

*Open mind* =
*acceptance, love, respect & possibilities.*

*Let's be open together!*
- Amy Wise

The path we
*choose*
is the *life*
we lead.

*Choose*
**wisely.**
—Amy Wise

Lessons from our past mold our present and create our future.
Learn, grow, thrive.

— Amy Wise

Karma is on the menu today.
Pay it forward and
enjoy the deliciousness!

—Amy Wise

If you stay in a comfort zone
too long, you can end up
in a stuck zone.

Get a little uncomfortable....
it will feel great!

– Amy Wise

# Dreams
### don't happen overnight,
### but they do happen.

Get up, get out, get going. . . .

## YOUR dreams
### are waiting!

- Amy Wise

Staying stale
or starting
fresh?
You choose.
- Amy Wise

A balanced life is a full life.....
have faith,
be thankful;
ask for help, give to others;
work hard, take breaks;
always learn, share knowledge;
dream, create; love,
love some more!

~Amy Wise

Mountains are meant to be climbed,
hurdles are meant to be jumped,
challenges are meant to be overcome,
obstacles are meant to be moved
and dreams are meant to
be real!

- Amy Wise

Once your dream
comes true;
turn around,
step back,
remember what
it was like getting there,
grab someone's
hand and help them
reach their dream.
- Amy Wise

Family and friends
            are seeds for the heart.
Faith and beliefs
            are seeds for the soul.
Dreams and goals
            are seeds for the mind.
Water them all and watch life GROW!
                        - Amy Wise

Lifting up,
    lending a hand,
and reaching out...
    can be a daily habit...
if we all just
    make it one.
            - Amy Wise

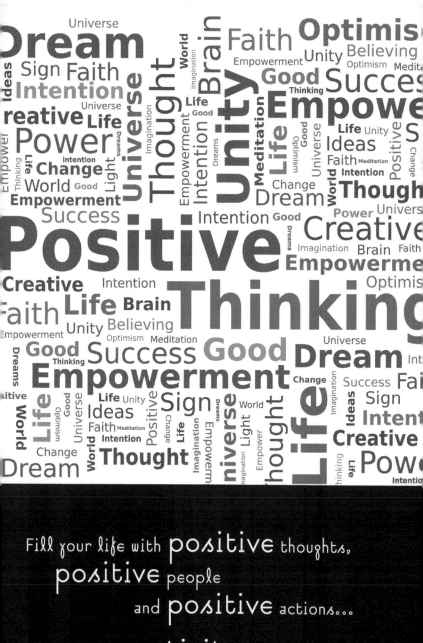

Fill your life with positive thoughts, positive people and positive actions...

then watch negativity quickly become a thing of the past!

— Amy Wise

we're all in this together,
even if we're on
different sides.
Let's meet in the middle and
**rock the world!**

- Amy Wise

When your dreams come true,
that's just the beginning.
Next, work hard to
make them the best they can be.
Then, pass the wisdom on
so someone else can do the same.

-Amy Wise

There is no *less*
when you know
you're worth
*MORE!*

—Amy Wise

When you start believing in
YOURSELF and that NOTHING
is impossible...
that's YOUR defining moment when
EVERYTHING becomes possible!

Believe!

-Amy Wise

Paying it forward
is the best way to
ensure everyone is
taken care of.

– Amy Wise

VOLUNTEER

Circumstances
don't shape
you,
you do.

~ Amy Wise

Who says
you can't?

YOU so can!

- Amy Wise

live your best life
by dreaming big,
Reaching for the stars,
loving hard, giving more
and appreciating it all.
-amy wise

108

For putting people
on "A" lists
and "D" lists
society should
get an "F."

Last I checked...
we're all **equal**.

— Amy Wise

God
Respect
Appreciation
Truth
Excellence
Family
Unity
Love
- Amy Wise

It's not about **me**,
　　　it's not about **you**,
it's about all of us...
　　　**together!**

– Amy Wise

# YES
## You can

Be your own
champion.
Believe in yourself.
Live YOUR passion.
Achieve YOUR dreams.
Because YOU CAN!!
- Amy Wise

When life takes an
**unexpected turn...**
don't look back...
**move forward**
in awe of the
**possibilities ahead.**

– Amy Wise

If there are **missing pieces** in your "**life's puzzle**," don't try to find them, start a "**new puzzle**" and watch with amazement as your **true meaning unfolds.**

– Amy Wise

There's an obstacle in your way?
Move it,
walk around it,
jump over it or
crawl under it...
now look back and know you're
stronger because of it.

— Amy Wise

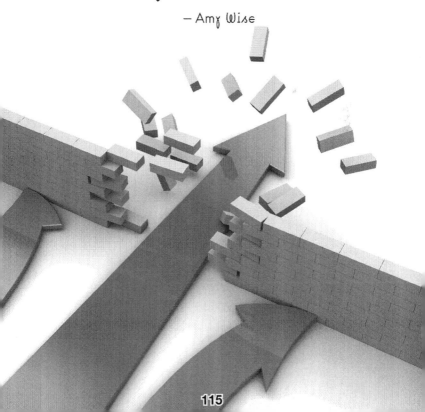

*Love* doesn't *feel* race, religion,
sexual orientation, class, education
or background.

*Love DOES feel* warmth, joy,
kindness, respect, passion, generosity,
compromise and communication.

*Love is so darn smart!*

- Amy Wise

Nobody's perfect, but we're ALL fabulous!

– Amy Wise

Don't just daydream...

LIVE YOUR DREAM!

- Amy Wise

Just because you can't reach it, doesn't mean you can't achieve it.

Stretch!

*Amy Wise*

Giving
is
your
heart's gift.

- Amy Wise

Without risk there is no change.
Without learning
there is no growth.
Without dreams there is no joy.
Live your best life.
Take a chance. *Now.*

— Amy Wise

Once you ask,
*believe*
and receive...
make sure you
*advise, teach,*
and *help.*

- Amy Wise

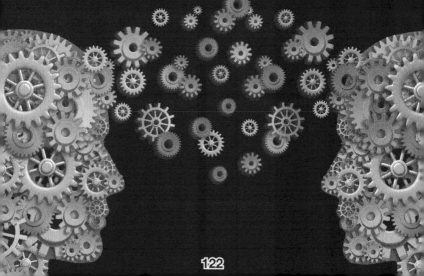

*Hurdles are temporary.*
*Faith is forever.*

- Amy Wise

Live your life
and when you
least expect it
the best person
for you will
become part of it.

-Amy Wise

When it comes to
*YOUR dreams...*
don't follow society,
don't follow your friends,
don't follow your parents,
don't follow the media...
*DO follow YOUR heart!*

~ Amy Wise

if we take care of
one another, then
we're all taken care of.

-amy wise

If you're
**shining bright,**
don't forget to be
someone else's
**light** during their
**dark time.**

— Amy Wise

Don't lose hope...
have faith.
Don't stay silent...
speak up.
Don't sit still....
take action.

— Amy Wise

Starting today make it a habit to:
Dream more.
Believe more.
Give more.
Help more.
Communicate more.
Understand more.
Appreciate more.
Learn more.
Teach more.
Be open to more.
Share more.
Lend more.
Love more!
–Amy Wise

Look back
and learn.
Look forward
and anticipate.

But most importantly...
look around
and live!

~Amy Wise

DON'T JUST
WALK AWAY
FROM YOUR
COMFORT
ZONE...
RUN!

-AMY WISE

If everyone
helps a little,
then nobody would
need a lot.

- Amy Wise

True **success**
comes from a *full soul*
and *happy heart.*

*- Amy Wise*

Giving
is a
way
of living.

- Amy Wise

When we *encourage* each other,
we have the *courage*
to let go of the *"me"*
and the *heart* to embrace
the *"we."* – Amy Wise

SILENCE

Silence isn't golden
if it prevents you from
standing up for what
you believe in.

— Amy Wise

# Mistakes
# + Lessons
---
# = **Growth**

– Amy Wise

Take a dream and make it come true. Actually... take as many dreams as you want and make them come true!

– Amy Wise

Even when the
*"rollercoaster ride"*
seems like it's never going to end,
just remember,
every **twist** and **turn** shapes us
into who we are today.
**Enjoy the ride!**

-Amy Wise

When we turn a
*blind eye* everyone hurts.
When we
open our eyes
everyone heals.

There are
no strangers,
we're all in this
together!

-Amy Wise

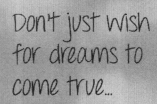

Don't just wish
for dreams to
come true...

CREATE!

Don't just smile when
you're doing what
you love...

LAUGH!

Don't wait
one more day...

GO!

-Amy Wise

Miracles happen when you believe they will. So starting today... BELIEVE!
- Amy Wise

When you treasure yourself, that's all the wealth you need. When you believe in yourself, you CAN achieve anything. When you're comfortable in your own skin, your beauty shines from your heart. When you realize this, you truly know you're enough!

– Amy Wise

Equality doesn't distinguish who is equal...

black, white, brown, straight, gay, Christian, Muslim, Jewish, Buddhist, Mormon, homeless, jobless, CEO, homeowner, man, woman, rich or poor...

equality means EVERYONE is equal.

– Amy Wise

If you stay **strong** in your **beliefs**,
work hard toward your **dreams**,
surround yourself with **positive people**,
follow your **heart**
and ALWAYS lend a hand...
you're **golden**.

\- Amy Wise

Look back for just a minute.
Okay, now look in the mirror
and see how far you've come.
Amazing huh!?
Be proud, keep growing
and just imagine
what the future holds!

- Amy Wise

Dream.
Believe.
Do.
You Can!

*- Amy Wise*

DREAM AVE

BELIEVE ST

Love isn't diamonds, roses and dinners.
Love is communication,
        understanding and partnership.
Love isn't selfish, cruel or hurtful.
Love is compromise, trust and honesty.

Love is lasting
    when it's for the right reasons.

- Amy Wise

It's not about how much, or how big, or who sees...
it's about every small gesture adding up to

a whole lot of good!

- Amy Wise

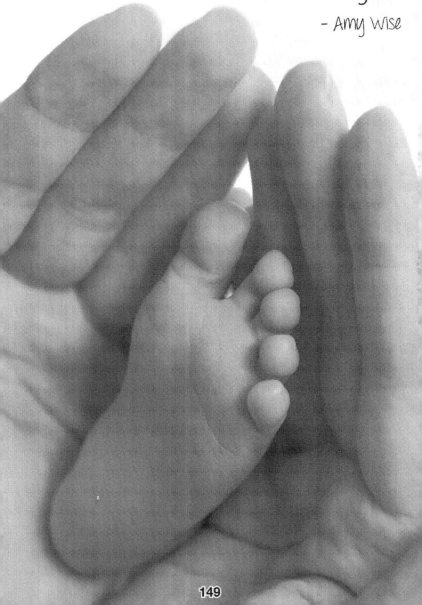

Dream big, have faith, learn from mistakes,
work hard, think positive, never give up,
believe in yourself...
    and then...
**watch miracles unfold,
    right before your eyes!**
        - Amy Wise

150

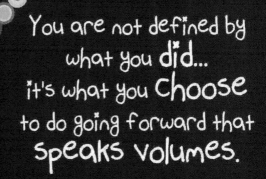

You are not defined by
what you **did**...
it's what you **choose**
to do going forward that
**speaks volumes.**

– Amy Wise

Tomorrow
Tomorrow
Tomorrow
TODAY
Yesterday

Let go of the past.

Don't try to predict
the future.

Give your
entire heart
to the present.

— Amy Wise

The roughest roads
will take you to the most
extraordinary places!

– Amy Wise

Rough Road
Just Ahead

Dreams become reality
when YOU
decide they
can!

-Amy Wise

Take a moment...
look around...
and be thankful...
for everything.

– Amy Wise

thank you

Lastly, whatever you do,
don't ever forget to...
Believe in yourself ~
Inspire others ~
Spread joy!

– Amy Wise

# About the Author

**Amy Wise** is an author, editor, blogger and philanthropist.

She is the author of the upcoming book, *This is Me....Coming Out of the Darkness* (2012), and is also working on a movie based on the same book. She is a contributing author in the anthologies; *Dancing at the Shame Prom* (Fall, 2012) and *Oil and Water and Other Things That Don't Mix* (2010).

Additionally she is the creator of *The Many Shades of Love* blog, www.themanyshadesoflove.blogspot.com where she writes about the ups and downs of being in an interracial marriage and family. She is a contributing writer for *TheNextFamily.com* online magazine, *EmbraceUS Multicultural Magazine* and the *Oil and Water* blog. Previously she wrote for *Adaptu.com* where her stories were about making it through financially hard times.

Amy also writes as a guest writer for various websites, blogs, and newspapers and is a ghost writer and editor for all genres of writers. She recently edited, *The Eat From Home Diet: How to Get a Slim Body and Fat Wallet* (2012).

She lives in sunny Chula Vista, CA with her husband Jamie and daughter Tatiana. She is forever passionate about helping others find their joy.

# —Connect with Amy—

Website: amywisewriter.com
Blog: themanyshadesoflove.blogspot.com
Email: amy@amywisewriter.com
Facebook: facebook.com/AmyWiseWriter

---

# Photo Credits

# Photo Credits

Page 85, ©Mikael Damkier, 2012
Page 86, ©Piko72, 2012
Page 87, ©AXL, 2012
Page 88, ©Andrea Danti, 2012
Page 89, ©Robert F. Balazik, 2012
Page 90, ©Lindwa, 2012
Page 91, ©Fra73, 2012
Page 92, ©Martin Novak, 2012
Page 93, ©Losevsky Pavel, 2012
Page 94, ©Liv friis-larsen, 2012
Page 95, ©Anatoli Styf, 2012
Page 96, ©drdre, 2012
Page 97, ©Santhosh Kumar, 2012
Page 98, ©Gyuszkofoto, 2012
Page 99, ©debra hughes, 2012
Page 100, ©artellia, 2012
Page 101, ©David Arts, 2012
Page 102, ©Dmitrijs Mihejevs, 2012
Page 103, ©Bruce Rolff, 2012
Page 104, ©Pixel 4 Images, 2012
Page 105, ©mangostock, 2012
Page 106, ©Joy Stein, 2012
Page 107, ©jorgen mcleman, 2012
Page 108, ©Cindy Hughes, 2012
Page 109, ©Bonita R. Cheshier, 2012
Page 110, ©mrpuiii, 2012
Page 111, ©Morgan DDL, 2012
Page 112, ©Raywoo, 2012
Page 113, ©photogl, 2012
Page 114, ©almagami, 2012
Page 115, ©mmaxer, 2012
Page 116, ©antoniomas, 2012
Page 117, ©Yaro, 2012
Page 118, ©Blend Images, 2012
Page 119, ©Dudarev Mikhail, 2012
Page 120, ©djgis, 2012
Page 121, ©benng, 2012
Page 122, ©Lightspring, 2012
Page 123, ©Milos Jaric, 2012
Page 124, ©Ivelin Radkov, 2012
Page 125, ©iQoncept, 2012
Page 126, ©Melissa King, 2012
Page 127, ©SkillUp, 2012
Page 128, ©Gordana Simic, 2012

Page 129, ©Oliko, 2012
Page 130, ©ARENA Creative, 2012
Page 131, ©Maridav, 2012
Page 132, ©ankur patil, 2012
Page 133, ©Sergej Razvodovskij, 2012
Page 134, ©EdBockStock, 2012
Page 135, ©ink tear, 2012
Page 136, ©Kalim, 2012
Page 137, ©Slavoljub Pantelic, 2012
Page 138, ©Lukiyanova Natalia / frenta, 2012
Page 139, ©Atlaspix, 2012
Page 140, ©Antonova Elena, 2012
Page 141, ©jokerpro, 2012
Page 142, ©Doreen Salcher, 2012
Page 143, ©Lia Koltyrina, 2012
Page 144, ©maxstockphoto, 2012
Page 145, ©KamiGami, 2012
Page 146, ©Yeko Photo Studio, 2012
Page 147, ©SVLuma, 2012
Page 148, ©ivylingpy, 2012
Page 149, ©Vadim Kolobanov, 2012
Page 150, ©Graphic design, 2012
Page 151, ©Michael Monahan, 2012
Page 152, ©Anson0618, 2012
Page 153, ©Andy Dean Photography, 2012
Page 154, ©Nemeziya, 2012
Page 155, ©design36, 2012
Page 156, ©irmus, 2012
Cover, ©blinkblink, 2012
Dedication, ©nuttapong, 2012

All photos used under license from Shutterstock.com.

# Notes

# Notes

14768272R00089

Made in the USA
Lexington, KY
18 April 2012